IMPULSE PURCHASING

by

Lalit Mohanty

PREFACE

This book aims to provide a comprehensive exploration of impulse purchasing, covering its psychological, societal, and cultural aspects. It also offers practical insights into managing and, when necessary, resisting the impulse to buy. Throughout the chapters, readers will gain a deeper understanding of the forces at play and find strategies to navigate the complex world of impulsive decision-making.

Table of Contents

Chapter 21: The Ethical Dimensions of Impulse Selling

Balancing Profit and Responsibility

Chapter 22: Marketing to the Mindful Consumer

Shifting Trends in Consumer Behavior

Chapter 23: The Role of Technology in Impulse Purchasing

From Augmented Reality to Virtual Carts

Chapter 24: Education and Impulse Control

Impulse Management as a Life Skill

Chapter 25: The Future of Impulse Purchasing

Predicting Trends and Adapting Strategies

CHAPTER 1

THE SIREN'S CALL

Understanding the Allure of Impulse Purchasing

The modern marketplace is a captivating symphony of colors, sounds, and sensations designed to lure us into a world of desires we never knew we had. In this retail orchestra, the Siren's call of impulse purchasing is a melody that resonates with the deepest recesses of our consumerist hearts.

1.1 The Allure of Instant Gratification

At its core, impulse purchasing is about the pursuit of instant gratification. The tantalizing prospect of possessing something new and exciting immediately captivates our senses. It's the promise of a quick fix to lift our spirits, to momentarily transcend the mundane, and to fill a void we may not even be consciously aware of.

1.2 The Temptation of Novelty

The Siren's call often whispers in the language of novelty. Whether it's the latest gadget, a limited edition item, or a trendy fashion piece, the allure lies in the freshness and uniqueness of the purchase. The idea that we are among the first to possess something novel feeds into our desire for social recognition and a sense of exclusivity.

1.3 The Illusion of Control

Impulse purchasing provides an illusion of control in a world that can often feel chaotic and unpredictable. In that fleeting moment of decision, we become the masters of our own destiny, choosing to indulge in something that brings us pleasure. This sense of control, however fleeting, is a powerful motivator, and the Siren's call capitalizes on our innate need to feel in charge.

1.4 The Emotional Connection

The Siren's call is an emotional one. It tugs at our heartstrings, leveraging the potent connection between emotions and buying behavior. Whether it's the joy of acquisition, the thrill of discovery, or the satisfaction of treating oneself, emotions play a pivotal role in the impulsive dance between the consumer and the marketplace.

1.5 The Influence of External Triggers

External stimuli often act as the Siren's call, beckoning us towards impulsive decisions. Cleverly crafted advertisements, strategically placed products, and limited-time offers are like musical notes in the symphony of consumerism, orchestrating a compelling narrative that urges us to succumb to the desire of the moment.

1.6 The Confluence of Urgency and Scarcity

The Siren's call is at its most persuasive when urgency and scarcity converge. Limited-time sales, one-of-a-kind deals, and exclusive offers create a sense of urgency, pushing us to make a decision swiftly before the opportunity slips away. The scarcity principle, emphasizing the rarity of an item, further intensifies the allure, making the purchase seem like a once-in-a-lifetime opportunity.

1.7 The Unconscious Urge

In the face of the Siren's call, our decision-making often operates on autopilot. Impulse purchasing exploits the subtle dance between our conscious and unconscious minds, leading us to make choices driven by instinct rather than careful consideration. Understanding this interplay is crucial in unraveling the mystery behind our impulsive tendencies.

In this chapter, we embark on a journey to comprehend the enchanting allure of impulse purchasing—the Siren's call that beckons us to navigate the labyrinth of desires and decisions. As we delve deeper into the psychological underpinnings, emotional triggers, and external influences, we equip ourselves with the knowledge needed to navigate the seductive currents of the consumerist sea.

CHAPTER 2

THE PSYCHOLOGY BEHIND IMPULSE BUYING

Delving into the Human Mind

The intricate dance of impulse buying unfolds within the theater of the human mind, a complex stage where emotions, desires, and cognitive processes converge. In this chapter, we embark on a journey into the depths of psychology, unraveling the mysteries behind the impulsive decisions that shape our consumer landscape.

2.1 The Role of Emotions

At the heart of impulse buying lies the intricate interplay of emotions. Our emotional responses, whether triggered by a sense of excitement, happiness, or even stress, significantly influence our purchasing decisions. Understanding the emotional currents that propel impulsive actions is key to deciphering the psychology at play.

2.2 Instant Gratification vs. Delayed Reward

The human brain is wired to seek immediate rewards, a trait deeply rooted in our evolutionary history. Impulse buying taps into this desire for instant gratification, offering a quick and tangible reward that trumps the prospect of delayed satisfaction. Exploring the neurological mechanisms behind this preference sheds light on the impulsive mindset.

2.3 The Dopamine Rush

Dopamine, often referred to as the "feel-good" neurotransmitter, takes center stage in the psychology of impulse buying. The anticipation of a rewarding purchase triggers a surge of dopamine, creating a pleasurable sensation that motivates us to repeat the behavior. Understanding this neurochemical dance provides insight into the addictive nature of impulsive decisions.

2.4 The Influence of Cognitive Biases

Our minds are susceptible to cognitive biases that can sway our decisions in unpredictable ways. From the anchoring effect to the scarcity heuristic, cognitive biases play a pivotal role in shaping the thought processes that lead to impulsive purchases. Exploring these biases offers a glimpse into the subconscious forces guiding our choices.

2.5 The Impulse Control Struggle

Impulse buying often involves a battle between the impulsive, pleasure-seeking self and the rational, self-disciplined self. This internal struggle is rooted in the psychological concept of self-control. Understanding how our minds grapple with the tension between immediate desires and long-term goals unveils the psychological complexities inherent in impulsive decision-making.

2.6 The Influence of Social Norms

Human beings are inherently social creatures, and our behaviors are often shaped by societal norms and expectations. The psychology of impulse buying is intertwined with the desire for social validation and conformity. Analyzing the impact of social influences provides a lens through which we can comprehend the communal aspects of impulsive behavior.

2.7 The Role of Personal Identity

Our self-perception and personal identity play a significant role in the psychology of impulse buying. Purchases can become symbolic expressions of our identity, contributing to a sense of self-worth and validation. Exploring how consumer choices intertwine with personal identity sheds light on the deeper motivations driving impulsive actions.

2.8 The Impact of Stress and Coping Mechanisms

Stress, a ubiquitous aspect of human existence, can act as both a catalyst and a deterrent to impulse buying. Understanding the role of stress in triggering impulsive behavior, as well as the coping mechanisms individuals employ, provides a nuanced perspective on the psychological dynamics at play.

2.9 The Unconscious Mind and Priming Effects

Much of our decision-making occurs at a subconscious level, influenced by priming effects that shape our perceptions and preferences. Unraveling the mysteries of the unconscious mind and its susceptibility to external cues unveils the subtleties that contribute to impulsive purchasing.

CHAPTER 3

THE IMPULSE PURCHASE
SPECTRUM

From Minor Splurges to Major Regrets

Impulse purchasing is not a monolithic phenomenon but rather a spectrum that spans from momentary indulgences to significant financial decisions. In this chapter, we navigate the diverse landscape of impulsive actions, exploring the spectrum that ranges from minor splurges to major regrets.

3.1 The Minor Splurges: Everyday Temptations

At the lower end of the spectrum lie the minor splurges—innocuous, often inexpensive purchases that bring a brief moment of joy. These can range from a decadent coffee on the way to work to an unplanned magazine at the checkout counter. While seemingly harmless, these minor indulgences contribute to the cumulative impact of impulse buying.

3.2 The Moderate Impulses: Spontaneous Treats

Moving along the spectrum, we encounter moderate impulses—impromptu purchases that surpass the realm of everyday temptations. These might include a spontaneous dinner at a favorite restaurant or an unplanned shopping spree during a weekend outing. The line between a minor splurge and a moderate impulse is blurred, emphasizing the subjective nature of impulse buying.

3.3 The Significant Splurges: Navigating the Gray Area

As we ascend the spectrum, the purchases become more substantial, blurring the line between momentary indulgence and considered decision-making. Significant splurges can range from a high-end gadget purchased on a whim to an impulsive weekend getaway. The financial impact of these decisions elevates the stakes and prompts reflection on the impulsive tendencies that lead to them.

3.4 The Major Regrets: When Impulse Turns Sour

At the upper end of the spectrum lie the major regrets—impulsive decisions with enduring consequences. These purchases, often fueled by a perfect storm of emotional triggers and external influences, can lead to significant financial strain and emotional turmoil. Examples include impulsively financing a luxury car or making a large investment without careful consideration.

3.5 The Continuum of Consequences

Understanding the impulse purchase spectrum requires acknowledging the continuum of consequences. Minor splurges may have negligible repercussions, while major regrets can reshape financial trajectories. Navigating this spectrum involves recognizing that the allure of impulse buying extends beyond the moment of purchase, with consequences rippling into the weeks, months, and even years that follow.

3.6 The Gradual Escalation of Impulsive Behavior

Individuals often find themselves on different points of the spectrum at different times in their lives. The progression from minor splurges to major regrets is not always linear but can represent a gradual escalation of impulsive behavior. Recognizing this progression is crucial for implementing effective strategies to curb impulsive tendencies.

3.7 Strategies for Mitigating Impulse Buying Across the Spectrum

Arming ourselves with strategies to navigate the impulse purchase spectrum is essential. From setting budgetary constraints for minor splurges to implementing cooling-off periods for significant purchases, individuals can adopt personalized approaches to curb impulsive behavior at various points along the spectrum. This chapter explores practical strategies that empower consumers to make more deliberate choices, irrespective of where they find themselves on the impulse purchase spectrum.

By dissecting the impulse purchase spectrum, we gain a nuanced understanding of the varied manifestations of impulsive behavior. Recognizing the spectrum's breadth equips us with the insight needed to implement tailored strategies, fostering a healthier relationship with our consumer impulses and mitigating the potential pitfalls that lie along the continuum.

CHAPTER 4

THE RISE OF IMPULSE CULTURE

How Society Fuels Impulsive Behavior

In the ever-evolving landscape of consumerism, the phenomenon of impulse buying is not merely an individual proclivity but a cultural force with deep-seated roots. This chapter explores the societal currents that contribute to the rise of an impulse culture, where the allure of instant gratification permeates every facet of our daily lives.

4.1 The Acceleration of Pace

Modern society operates at an unprecedented pace, driven by technological advancements and a relentless pursuit of efficiency. The resulting acceleration of daily life leaves individuals craving instant solutions and quick fixes. In this context, impulse buying becomes a convenient and immediate means of gratification, aligning seamlessly with the accelerated pace of contemporary living.

4.2 The Influence of Social Media

Social media platforms act as potent catalysts in the propagation of impulse culture. The constant stream of curated content, targeted advertisements, and influencers showcasing the latest trends creates an environment where the desire to keep up with the ever-changing landscape of consumerism becomes overwhelming. The "fear of missing out" (FOMO) is amplified, compelling individuals to make impulsive purchases to stay in sync with their online peers.

4.3 E-Commerce and One-Click Convenience

The advent of e-commerce has revolutionized the way we shop, offering unparalleled convenience at the click of a button. While this convenience streamlines the purchasing process, it also lowers the barriers to impulsive buying. With one-click purchasing options and personalized recommendations, e-commerce platforms create an environment conducive to quick, spur-of-the-moment decisions.

4.4 Marketing Strategies: Creating Urgency and Scarcity

Marketers play a pivotal role in shaping impulse culture through the strategic deployment of urgency and scarcity. Limited-time offers, flash sales, and exclusive deals create an atmosphere where consumers feel compelled to act swiftly to secure a perceived advantage. The fear of missing out on a unique opportunity becomes a powerful motivator, driving impulsive purchases.

4.5 The Disposable Culture Phenomenon

The rise of a disposable culture, characterized by the rapid turnover of goods and a focus on trends, fuels impulsive behavior. The notion that products have a short lifespan and will soon be replaced by newer, more enticing alternatives encourages consumers to make impulsive purchases without considering the long-term implications of their buying decisions.

4.6 Peer Influence and Social Validation

In an interconnected world, peer influence and social validation play a significant role in shaping consumer behavior. The constant exposure to the lifestyles of others, fueled by social media, creates a desire for validation through possessions. Impulse buying becomes a means of attaining social recognition and affirming one's place in a perceived hierarchy of status and success.

4.7 The Accessibility of Credit

Easy access to credit amplifies the culture of impulse buying. Credit cards and buy-now-pay-later options provide immediate purchasing power, dissociating the act of buying from the immediate impact on one's finances. The deferred consequences of impulsive purchases contribute to a cycle of debt that can be challenging to break.

4.8 The Impact of Consumerism on Identity

In a consumer-driven society, possessions are often intertwined with identity. The constant bombardment of advertisements and societal expectations fosters a culture where individuals derive a sense of self-worth from their material acquisitions. This connection between consumerism and identity reinforces the impulse to make purchases based on emotional fulfillment and validation.

Understanding the societal forces that fuel impulse culture is essential for individuals seeking to navigate the consumer landscape consciously. As we dissect the intricate web of influences—from the accelerated pace of life to the pervasive reach of social media—we gain insights into the collective factors that contribute to the rise of impulse behavior in our culture. This awareness serves as a foundation for developing strategies to foster mindful consumption in an environment that often encourages the opposite.

CHAPTER 5

THE RETAILER'S PLAYGROUND

Strategies to Entice Impulse Purchases

In the dynamic arena of retail, every storefront, whether physical or virtual, is a carefully crafted stage. Within this playground, retailers employ a myriad of strategies to engage consumers and coax them into spontaneous purchasing decisions. This chapter unveils the tactics and techniques that transform a retail space into a realm where the siren song of impulse buying becomes irresistibly alluring.

5.1 Strategic Store Layouts

The physical layout of a store is a critical element in the retailer's arsenal. By strategically placing high-margin and visually appealing items at key focal points, retailers guide customers through carefully curated pathways. This deliberate orchestration nudges patrons towards unplanned purchases, leveraging the psychology of spatial design to stimulate impulsive behavior.

5.2 Eye-Catching Displays and Visual Merchandising

The power of aesthetics cannot be overstated in the retailer's playground. Eye-catching displays and visually enticing arrangements capture the attention of shoppers, drawing them towards featured products. Strategic lighting, bold colors, and artful presentation contribute to an environment that stimulates the senses, triggering impulsive responses to the allure of the merchandise.

5.3 Limited-Time Offers and Flash Sales

Creating a sense of urgency is a time-tested strategy to instigate impulsive purchases. Retailers introduce limited-time offers and flash sales, encouraging customers to act quickly to secure exclusive deals. The fear of missing out on a bargain propels individuals to make spontaneous decisions, contributing to the sense of excitement and immediacy in the shopping experience.

5.4 Strategic Pricing and Discounts

Pricing strategies play a pivotal role in shaping consumer behavior. Retailers employ tactics such as dynamic pricing, bundling, and tiered discounts to create the perception of value. The allure of a discounted item or a special offer can sway customers towards impulsive buying, as the appeal of perceived savings outweighs rational deliberation.

5.5 Cross-Selling and Upselling Techniques

Enticing customers to add complementary or upgraded items to their purchase is a classic technique in the retailer's playbook. Cross-selling and upselling capitalize on the customer's current buying mindset, suggesting additional items that enhance the shopping experience. These techniques subtly guide individuals towards expanding their initial purchase, increasing the overall transaction value.

5.6 Interactive and Experiential Retail Environments

Modern retailers are increasingly embracing interactive and experiential environments to captivate consumers. Hands-on displays, virtual reality experiences, and interactive elements create a dynamic and engaging atmosphere. In such settings, the lines between browsing and buying blur, fostering an environment where impulsive decisions feel natural and spontaneous.

5.7 Personalized Recommendations and Targeted Marketing

Advancements in data analytics enable retailers to tailor recommendations and marketing messages to individual preferences. Personalized suggestions, based on past purchases and browsing history, create a sense of intimacy between the consumer and the retailer. This personalization not only enhances the overall shopping experience but also increases the likelihood of impulsive purchases driven by a sense of familiarity and connection.

5.8 Convenient Checkout Processes

Streamlining the checkout process is a key strategy in facilitating impulse purchases. Whether in-store or online, retailers strive to minimize friction during the final stages of a transaction. One-click purchasing options, seamless payment gateways, and hassle-free returns reduce barriers, making impulsive decisions more enticing and effortless for consumers.

By unraveling the tactics employed in the retailer's playground, consumers gain a heightened awareness of the persuasive forces at play during the shopping experience. Recognizing these strategies empowers individuals to navigate retail spaces with a critical eye, making conscious choices amidst the carefully orchestrated dance designed to elicit impulsive responses.

CHAPTER 6

THE POWER OF PACKAGING

Unwrapping the Influence of Presentation

In the world of consumerism, the packaging of a product is not merely a protective shell; it is a powerful communicator, a silent influencer, and an artful orchestrator of perception. This chapter delves into the profound impact of packaging on consumer behavior, revealing how the external appearance of a product can cast an enchanting spell on the buyer and ignite the impulse to purchase.

6.1 The First Impression

The moment a product catches a consumer's eye, the packaging becomes the ambassador of the brand. The first impression is often visual, and a well-designed package has the potential to captivate attention amidst the sea of choices. Colors, typography, and imagery conspire to convey a message that resonates with the consumer's emotions and preferences.

6.2 The Psychology of Colors and Shapes

Colors and shapes embedded in packaging design wield a psychological influence that goes beyond aesthetics. Warm tones evoke feelings of comfort and familiarity, while bold and contrasting colors can convey excitement and vitality. Similarly, the shape of a package can elicit subconscious associations, influencing how a product is perceived and whether it triggers an impulse to buy.

6.3 Storytelling Through Design

Packaging is a silent storyteller, weaving narratives that resonate with the consumer's aspirations and desires. The imagery and text on a package create a visual narrative, communicating the brand's values, origin, or the unique story behind the product. This storytelling aspect adds depth to the consumer's experience, fostering a connection that transcends the functional purpose of the product.

6.4 The Perception of Quality

The quality of a product is often inferred from the quality of its packaging. Sleek, well-designed packaging communicates a sense of sophistication and attention to detail, influencing the perceived value of the item within. Consumers may find themselves drawn to products with packaging that suggests a premium or superior quality, even if the actual product merits are yet to be examined.

6.5 The Allure of Unboxing

The unboxing experience has become a cultural phenomenon, fueled by social media and the desire to share moments of excitement. Thoughtfully designed packaging that enhances the unboxing ritual elevates the overall product experience. Brands strategically utilize this phenomenon, creating anticipation and delight that amplify the consumer's emotional connection to the product.

6.6 The Role of Transparency and Sustainability

In an era of heightened environmental consciousness, packaging that communicates transparency and sustainability holds particular sway. Consumers are increasingly drawn to products with eco-friendly packaging, reflecting a commitment to environmental responsibility. The power of packaging extends beyond aesthetics to align with the values and ethical considerations of the modern consumer.

6.7 Subliminal Messages and Hidden Cues

Packaging design is rife with subliminal messages and hidden cues that tap into the consumer's subconscious. From subtle logos and brand motifs to strategically placed symbols, these elements influence perception without conscious awareness. Unraveling the layers of these hidden cues unveils the intricate dance between packaging design and impulsive decision-making.

6.8 The Influence of Limited Editions and Collectibles

Limited edition or collectible packaging creates a sense of exclusivity and urgency, enticing consumers to make impulsive purchases before the opportunity vanishes. Whether adorned with unique artwork, special editions, or commemorative designs, such packaging triggers a desire to possess a piece of something rare and fleeting.

Understanding the power of packaging provides consumers with a lens through which to decode the visual language that surrounds them. By unwrapping the influence of presentation, individuals can cultivate a discerning eye, recognizing the ways in which packaging design shapes their perceptions and influences the impulse to bring a product into their lives.

CHAPTER 7

THE DIGITAL TEMPTATION

Impulse Buying in the Age of E-Commerce

In the digital era, the landscape of commerce has undergone a transformative evolution. The rise of e-commerce has not only revolutionized the way we shop but has also introduced new dimensions to the allure of impulse buying. This chapter explores the unique challenges and opportunities presented by digital platforms, unraveling the digital temptation that beckons consumers to succumb to impulsive decisions in the virtual realm.

7.1 The Seamless Shopping Experience

E-commerce platforms have redefined convenience, offering a shopping experience that transcends physical boundaries. With a few clicks or taps, consumers can explore an extensive array of products, compare prices, and make purchases without leaving the comfort of their homes. The seamless nature of online shopping minimizes barriers and accelerates the path from desire to transaction, fostering an environment ripe for impulsive behavior.

7.2 Personalized Recommendations and Algorithms

The digital realm is powered by algorithms that analyze user behavior, preferences, and past purchases to generate personalized recommendations. While this customization enhances the user experience, it also serves as a double-edged sword, as tailored suggestions can lead individuals down the path of impulsive buying. The temptation to explore and indulge in items that align with one's preferences becomes difficult to resist.

7.3 The Pervasiveness of Online Ads

Digital platforms inundate users with targeted advertisements, strategically placed to capture attention and stimulate desire. Whether on social media, search engines, or other online spaces, these ads are carefully crafted to appeal to specific demographics and interests. The constant exposure to enticing promotions contributes to the digital temptation, prompting users to click and make impulsive purchases.

7.4 Social Media Influencers and Shoppable Content

Social media influencers wield considerable influence in the digital realm. Through curated content and sponsored posts, they showcase products in aspirational scenarios, creating a narrative that resonates with their followers. Shoppable content further blurs the lines between discovery and purchase, allowing users to seamlessly transition from inspiration to acquisition with a simple tap.

7.5 The Rise of Flash Sales and Daily Deals

Digital platforms excel in creating a sense of urgency through flash sales and daily deals. Limited-time offers, countdowns, and exclusive promotions fuel the fear of missing out (FOMO), compelling consumers to make impulsive decisions before the opportunity vanishes. The constant availability of such time-sensitive opportunities heightens the digital temptation to act quickly.

7.6 Reviews and Social Proof

The digital realm facilitates the rapid dissemination of user reviews and social proof. The opinions and experiences of other consumers, easily accessible at the click of a button, influence the decision-making process. Positive reviews and endorsements create a sense of trust and validation, nudging individuals towards impulsive purchases based on the shared satisfaction of others.

7.7 Gamification of Shopping

Digital platforms often incorporate elements of gamification into the shopping experience. Loyalty programs, reward points, and interactive features create a sense of fun and excitement, turning the act of shopping into an engaging game. The thrill of accumulating points or unlocking exclusive perks becomes a powerful motivator, contributing to impulsive decisions in the pursuit of rewards.

7.8 The 24/7 Accessibility Dilemma

E-commerce operates around the clock, offering unparalleled accessibility. While this convenience is a hallmark of digital shopping, it also presents a challenge in terms of impulse control. The constant availability of products and the ability to shop at any hour contribute to impulsive decisions, as the barriers of time and location are dismantled.

Navigating the digital temptation requires a heightened awareness of the unique dynamics at play in the online shopping landscape. By understanding the influence of personalized algorithms, targeted ads, and the gamification of e-commerce, consumers can equip themselves with the tools needed to make intentional choices amidst the digital allure of impulsive buying.

CHAPTER 8

THE SOCIAL MEDIA SPIRAL

From Scrolling to Checkout in Seconds

In the interconnected world of social media, the journey from casual scrolling to completing a purchase has become a seamless, almost instantaneous process. This chapter explores the intricate dynamics of the social media spiral, unraveling how platforms designed for connection have become powerful catalysts for impulsive buying, taking users from idle scrolling to the checkout page in a matter of seconds.

8.1 The Scroll and Discover Culture

Social media platforms thrive on a culture of endless scrolling and content discovery. Users are presented with a continuous stream of images, videos, and posts, fostering an environment where the next enticing discovery is only a swipe or click away. This constant exposure sets the stage for impulsive behavior, as users encounter a myriad of products seamlessly integrated into their feeds.

8.2 Influencers as Shopping Guides

Social media influencers wield considerable influence as they bridge the gap between content creation and commerce. By seamlessly integrating product recommendations into their content, influencers become virtual shopping guides. The authenticity and relatability they project contribute to the social media spiral, transforming casual followers into impulsive buyers eager to emulate the lifestyles they admire.

8.3 Shoppable Posts and Instant Gratification

The integration of shoppable posts transforms social media platforms into virtual storefronts. Users can now explore products showcased in posts and, with a few clicks, transition from admiration to ownership. This immediate access to purchase options aligns with the culture of instant gratification, propelling users further into the social media spiral by reducing the friction between desire and fulfillment.

8.4 Social Commerce and Peer Influence

Social commerce, the convergence of e-commerce and social media, leverages the power of peer influence. Recommendations, reviews, and user-generated content create a communal shopping experience. The sense of camaraderie and shared experiences fostered by social platforms amplifies the desire to participate, encouraging users to make impulsive purchases to be part of the collective narrative.

8.5 FOMO and Limited-Time Offers

The fear of missing out (FOMO) is a potent force in the social media spiral. Limited-time offers and exclusive promotions capitalize on this fear, compelling users to act swiftly to secure a perceived advantage. Scrolling through a feed becomes a race against time, with impulsive decisions driven by the urgency to participate in a fleeting opportunity.

8.6 Social Proof and Validation

Social media platforms are hubs of social validation, where users seek recognition and approval. The public display of purchases, whether through unboxing videos, hauls, or tagged photos, serves as a form of social proof. The desire for validation fuels the social media spiral, as users make impulsive purchases driven by the prospect of positive attention and affirmation from their online community.

8.7 Retargeting and Persistent Presence

The social media spiral is further fueled by retargeting strategies that ensure a product stays within a user's digital orbit. Advertisements for products previously viewed linger across various platforms, maintaining a persistent presence. This continuous exposure heightens the likelihood of an impulsive decision, as the product becomes a familiar and tempting presence in the user's digital landscape.

8.8 Balancing Connectivity and Consumerism

Navigating the social media spiral requires a delicate balance between connectivity and consumerism. As social platforms seamlessly integrate shopping experiences, users must cultivate awareness of the persuasive forces at play. By understanding the dynamics of influencer marketing, shoppable features, and the interplay of social dynamics, individuals can engage with social media mindfully, avoiding impulsive pitfalls and making intentional choices in the digital marketplace.

CHAPTER 9

THE ROLE OF DISCOUNTS AND PROMOTIONS

How Sales Propel Impulse Purchases

Discounts and promotions are potent tools in the arsenal of retailers, capable of turning a casual shopper into an impulsive buyer in the blink of an eye. This chapter delves into the psychology behind sales strategies, exploring how the allure of discounts, limited-time offers, and promotions creates a compelling environment that propels consumers toward impulsive purchasing decisions.

9.1 The Psychological Appeal of Discounts

Discounts have a universal allure that transcends cultural and economic boundaries. The mere sight of a reduced price triggers a cascade of psychological responses. The perception of a good deal activates the brain's reward centers, releasing dopamine and creating a sense of pleasure and satisfaction. This emotional response forms the foundation of the impulsive buying triggered by discounts.

9.2 Limited-Time Offers and Urgency

The introduction of urgency through limited-time offers is a key element in the promotional playbook. The fear of missing out on a significant discount motivates consumers to act swiftly. Limited-time promotions create a sense of urgency that heightens emotional responses, pushing individuals to make impulsive decisions to secure the perceived benefits before time runs out.

9.3 Buy-One-Get-One (BOGO) and Bundling Tactics

The allure of getting more for the same price is a compelling force. Buy-One-Get-One (BOGO) offers and bundling tactics tap into the desire for added value. These promotions not only trigger the pleasure centers associated with discounts but also introduce an element of abundance, enticing consumers to make impulsive purchases driven by the prospect of getting more for their money.

9.4 Flash Sales and Exclusivity

Flash sales create an atmosphere of exclusivity and immediacy. By limiting the availability of discounted items for a short period, retailers magnify the sense of exclusivity. The swift nature of flash sales intensifies the impulse to buy, as consumers feel a heightened need to participate in an exclusive event and seize the opportunity before it vanishes.

9.5 Loyalty Programs and Reward Systems

Loyalty programs and reward systems introduce a gamified dimension to shopping. The promise of accumulating points, earning discounts, or unlocking exclusive perks fosters a sense of achievement and anticipation. The desire to attain these rewards becomes a powerful motivator, leading consumers to make impulsive purchases in pursuit of the perceived benefits offered by loyalty programs.

9.6 Psychological Pricing Strategies

The way prices are presented can significantly impact consumer perception. Psychological pricing strategies, such as pricing items at $9.99 instead of $10, create the illusion of a lower cost. The subtle manipulation of numbers plays on cognitive biases and influences the perceived value of a product, contributing to the impulsive decision to make a purchase.

9.7 Online Coupons and Digital Codes

In the digital age, the distribution of online coupons and promotional codes has become commonplace. The act of entering a code to unlock a discount triggers a sense of accomplishment and reward. This interactive element enhances the online shopping experience, creating a psychological connection between the effort exerted (entering the code) and the subsequent reward (discount), motivating impulsive decisions.

9.8 Social Media Promotions and Sharing Incentives

Promotions on social media platforms often come with sharing incentives. The prospect of additional discounts or exclusive deals for sharing a promotion with friends amplifies the social nature of impulsive buying. Consumers, driven by the desire to maximize their benefits, are enticed to make impulsive purchases and share the promotional content, perpetuating the cycle.

Understanding the role of discounts and promotions in impulse buying illuminates the intricate dance between consumer psychology and sales strategies. As consumers navigate the landscape of tempting offers, awareness of the emotional and cognitive triggers at play empowers them to make more intentional choices, balancing the desire for savings with the need for mindful consumption.

CHAPTER 10

IMPULSE PURCHASING AND EMOTIONS

Emotional Triggers and the Buying Frenzy

In the realm of impulse purchasing, emotions reign supreme, wielding a profound influence on the decisions we make as consumers. This chapter delves into the intricate interplay between emotions and impulsive buying, exploring how a myriad of feelings, from joy to stress, serves as catalysts for the buying frenzy that characterizes impulsive behavior.

10.1 The Emotional Landscape of Impulse Buying

At its core, impulse buying is an emotional endeavor. Whether driven by the thrill of discovery, the desire for comfort, or the pursuit of happiness, emotions play a pivotal role in shaping the impulsive decisions we make as consumers. Understanding the emotional landscape is key to unraveling the complexities of impulse purchasing.

10.2 The Joy of Acquisition

The joy of acquiring something new is a powerful emotional trigger. The anticipation leading up to a purchase, the act of possession, and the satisfaction derived from obtaining a desired item all contribute to a surge of positive emotions. Retailers capitalize on this joy by creating environments that amplify the pleasure associated with impulse buying.

10.3 Retail Therapy and Stress Relief

For many, shopping serves as a form of therapy, offering solace in times of stress or emotional distress. The act of purchasing provides a temporary escape from life's challenges, offering a sense of control and comfort. The emotional relief derived from retail therapy often drives impulsive decisions as individuals seek a quick and tangible remedy for their emotional state.

10.4 The Thrill of Discovery

The thrill of discovering something new and exciting is a compelling emotional trigger. Limited-time offers, exclusive deals, and novel products tap into the thrill of the chase. The excitement associated with the potential for a unique find fuels impulsive behavior, as consumers succumb to the allure of the unknown and the promise of a delightful surprise.

10.5 Nostalgia and Sentimental Attachments

Nostalgia holds a potent sway over consumer emotions. Products associated with memories, cultural references, or personal experiences evoke a sense of nostalgia, creating an emotional connection that transcends rational decision-making. Impulse buying driven by nostalgia is often fueled by the desire to recapture or recreate positive emotions from the past.

10.6 Fear of Missing Out (FOMO)

The fear of missing out is a powerful emotional motivator in the realm of impulse purchasing. Limited-time offers, exclusive promotions, and the anticipation of scarcity create a sense of urgency. The emotional discomfort associated with the prospect of missing out on a unique opportunity propels individuals to make impulsive decisions to avoid the perceived loss.

10.7 Guilt and the Need for Gratification

Feelings of guilt and the need for gratification are emotional triggers that drive impulsive behavior. The guilt associated with denying oneself a desired item can lead to impulsive purchases as a means of self-indulgence. The emotional gratification derived from the act of buying serves as a temporary salve for the internal conflict between desire and restraint.

10.8 Loneliness and the Urge for Connection

Loneliness can trigger the impulse to buy in an attempt to fill an emotional void. Products, especially those marketed as companions or sources of comfort, become appealing to individuals seeking a sense of connection. The emotional need for companionship and comfort often drives impulsive purchases as a means of alleviating loneliness.

10.9 Buyer's Remorse and Emotional Reckoning

The emotional journey of impulse buying extends beyond the moment of purchase. Buyer's remorse, the feeling of regret or anxiety following an impulsive decision, is a common emotional aftermath. The emotional reckoning that follows may prompt individuals to reflect on the underlying emotions that led to the impulsive purchase and reconsider their buying habits.

Understanding the intricate dance between emotions and impulse buying is crucial for individuals seeking to navigate the complex landscape of consumerism consciously. By recognizing the emotional triggers at play, consumers can develop strategies to cultivate emotional intelligence, make intentional choices, and foster a healthier relationship with the emotions that fuel the buying frenzy of impulse purchasing.

CHAPTER 11

THE AFTERMATH OF IMPULSE BUYING

Dealing with Buyer's Remorse

The exhilaration of an impulse purchase often gives way to a sobering reality—the aftermath of buyer's remorse. In this chapter, we explore the emotional and practical dimensions of coping with buyer's remorse, providing insights and strategies to navigate the aftermath of impulsive buying.

11.1 Understanding Buyer's Remorse

Buyer's remorse is a common emotional response characterized by feelings of regret, anxiety, or guilt after making a purchase. It emerges when the initial thrill of acquisition dissipates, and the consumer confronts the consequences of their impulsive decision.

Understanding the nature of buyer's remorse is the first step in managing its impact.

11.2 Reflecting on Impulsive Decisions

Upon experiencing buyer's remorse, reflection becomes a valuable tool. Consider the factors that led to the impulsive decision. Was it driven by a specific emotion, a desire for instant gratification, or external pressures? Reflecting on the root causes helps individuals gain insight into their impulsive tendencies and paves the way for more mindful decision-making in the future.

11.3 Embracing Emotional Resilience

Dealing with buyer's remorse requires emotional resilience. Acknowledge the feelings of regret without letting them spiral into self-criticism. Embrace the realization that everyone makes impulsive decisions at times, and it is a part of the learning process. Cultivating emotional resilience allows individuals to move forward with a constructive mindset.

11.4 The Art of Decision Reversal

In some cases, reversing an impulsive decision is a viable option. Check the retailer's return policy and explore the possibility of returning the item. Many businesses provide a window for returns or exchanges. Taking advantage of this option can alleviate the emotional burden associated with buyer's remorse and restore a sense of control.

11.5 Creating a Cooling-Off Period

Implementing a cooling-off period is a proactive strategy to prevent impulsive buying and minimize buyer's remorse. Before finalizing a purchase, step back and give yourself time to reflect. This intentional pause allows emotions to settle, providing clarity and enabling more rational decision-making. It serves as a buffer against the heat of the moment.

11.6 Establishing Budgetary Boundaries

Setting clear budgetary boundaries is a fundamental aspect of mitigating buyer's remorse. Establish limits on discretionary spending and allocate funds intentionally. Having a well-defined budget not only prevents impulsive purchases that may lead to regret but also fosters financial responsibility and long-term financial well-being.

11.7 Practicing Mindful Consumption

Mindful consumption is a holistic approach to managing impulsive buying and its aftermath. It involves cultivating awareness of one's values, needs, and the impact of purchasing decisions. Before making a purchase, ask yourself if it aligns with your values and contributes positively to your life. Mindful consumption encourages intentional choices and fosters a healthier relationship with material possessions.

11.8 Seeking Support and Accountability

Share your impulsive buying experiences with a trusted friend, family member, or mentor. Having a support system can provide emotional validation and practical advice. Furthermore, enlisting an accountability partner to share your financial goals and impulsive tendencies fosters a sense of responsibility and encourages more deliberate decision-making.

11.9 Learning and Growth

Embrace buyer's remorse as an opportunity for personal growth and learning. Every experience, even those tinged with regret, contributes to a deeper understanding of oneself. Use the lessons from impulsive buying episodes to refine decision-making skills, develop resilience, and cultivate a more intentional and conscious approach to consumption.

11.10 Professional Assistance and Financial Counseling

For individuals grappling with persistent impulsive buying habits and their financial repercussions, seeking professional assistance may be beneficial. Financial counselors and therapists specializing in behavioral finance can provide tailored strategies to address the emotional and financial aspects of impulsive buying, offering guidance for a more balanced and sustainable approach.

Navigating the aftermath of impulse buying involves a combination of self-reflection, intentional decision-making, and cultivating emotional resilience. By understanding the root causes of buyer's remorse and implementing proactive strategies, individuals can transform moments of regret into opportunities for personal growth, financial empowerment, and a more mindful approach to consumption.

CHAPTER 12

THE IMPULSE-RESISTANT CONSUMER

Strategies for Building Resistance

In a world where the allure of impulse buying is omnipresent, becoming an impulse-resistant consumer is a powerful skill. This chapter explores strategies and techniques to fortify yourself against the pull of impulsive purchases, empowering you to make intentional and mindful choices in the face of the myriad temptations presented by the consumer landscape.

12.1 Cultivating Financial Mindfulness

Financial mindfulness is the cornerstone of impulse resistance. Develop a keen awareness of your financial situation, including income, expenses, and savings goals. Regularly review your budget, track spending patterns, and consider the long-term impact of purchases. Cultivating financial mindfulness provides a solid foundation for making intentional and informed financial decisions.

12.2 Setting Clear Financial Goals

Establishing clear financial goals provides direction and purpose to your spending habits. Define short-term and long-term objectives, whether they involve saving for a vacation, building an emergency fund, or investing for the future. Aligning your purchases with these goals reinforces the importance of intentional spending and serves as a powerful deterrent against impulsive decisions.

12.3 Creating a Thoughtful Shopping List

Before embarking on a shopping expedition, whether in-store or online, create a thoughtful shopping list. List the items you genuinely need and prioritize them based on importance. Stick to the list, and avoid veering off course with unplanned purchases. This disciplined approach helps curb impulsive buying and promotes a more focused and purposeful shopping experience.

12.4 Implementing the 24-Hour Rule

Introduce a cooling-off period by adopting the 24-hour rule for significant purchases. When confronted with the temptation to make an impulsive buy, commit to waiting 24 hours before finalizing the decision. This time allows emotions to settle, providing a clearer perspective on the necessity and value of the purchase. Often, the initial urge diminishes during this waiting period.

12.5 Unsubscribing from Temptations

Take control of your digital environment by unsubscribing from promotional emails, newsletters, and notifications that trigger impulsive buying. Reduce exposure to online advertisements and social media content designed to incite desire. Streamlining your digital interactions minimizes external stimuli that contribute to impulsive behavior and supports the cultivation of intentional consumption.

12.6 Practicing Contentment and Gratitude

Cultivating a mindset of contentment and gratitude is a powerful antidote to the desire for constant acquisition. Reflect on the things you already possess and express gratitude for them. By appreciating what you have, you shift the focus from what is lacking, reducing the impulse to seek fulfillment through impulsive purchases.

12.7 Learning to Differentiate Wants from Needs

Distinguishing between wants and needs is crucial for impulse resistance. Before making a purchase, evaluate whether the item is a genuine necessity or a fleeting desire. Adopting a discerning mindset helps you prioritize essential purchases and reduces the likelihood of succumbing to impulsive buying fueled by momentary whims.

12.8 Engaging in Mindful Consumption Practices

Mindful consumption involves being fully present and conscious during the act of buying. Pay attention to your emotions, motivations, and the environmental cues that influence your decisions. Pause to evaluate the impact of a purchase on your well-being and the environment. Engaging in mindful consumption practices fosters a heightened awareness that promotes intentional and sustainable choices.

12.9 Establishing Accountability Partnerships

Share your journey towards impulse resistance with a trusted friend, family member, or colleague. Establishing an accountability partnership provides mutual support in navigating the challenges of consumerism. Share your financial goals, impulse-resistant strategies, and celebrate milestones together. The shared commitment to intentional consumption enhances resilience against impulsive buying.

12.10 Continuous Self-Education on Consumer Psychology

Stay informed about consumer psychology, marketing tactics, and the science behind impulse buying. Knowledge is a powerful tool for building resistance. Understanding the strategies employed by marketers equips you with the awareness to recognize and counteract their influence. Continuous self-education empowers you to make informed and intentional choices in the consumer landscape.

Becoming an impulse-resistant consumer is a journey that combines self-awareness, intentional decision-making, and a commitment to financial well-being. By implementing these strategies, you can fortify yourself against the allure of impulsive purchases, foster a mindful approach to consumption, and embark on a path towards a more intentional and empowered consumer lifestyle.

CHAPTER 13

THE IMPULSE PURCHASING PARADOX

Balancing Spontaneity and Fiscal Responsibility

The realm of impulse purchasing is marked by a paradox—an intricate dance between the spontaneity that makes life vibrant and the fiscal responsibility essential for financial well-being. In this chapter, we explore the delicate equilibrium required to navigate the impulse purchasing paradox, harmonizing the joy of spontaneity with the necessity of prudent financial management.

13.1 The Joys of Spontaneity

Spontaneity injects life with vibrancy, injecting unexpected moments of joy and excitement. Whether it's stumbling upon a quaint bookstore, discovering a unique piece of art, or trying a new cuisine, spontaneity enriches our experiences and adds color to the tapestry of life. Embracing the joy of the unexpected is an integral aspect of the human experience.

13.2 The Temptations of Impulse Buying

Yet, the same spontaneity that brings joy can also lead to impulsive decisions with financial consequences. The allure of a spontaneous purchase, driven by the thrill of the moment, can sometimes overshadow the need for fiscal responsibility. Balancing the joys of spontaneity with a mindful approach to spending is the crux of the impulse purchasing paradox.

13.3 Recognizing the Emotional Dynamics

At the heart of the paradox lies the recognition of emotional dynamics. Spontaneous purchases often arise from emotions like excitement, curiosity, or the desire for instant gratification. Acknowledging these emotional triggers is essential for navigating the paradox consciously. By understanding the emotional undercurrents, you can make more intentional choices in the moment.

13.4 Setting Spontaneity Parameters

Establishing parameters for spontaneity is a strategic approach to balance the paradox. Rather than eliminating spontaneous purchases altogether, set guidelines that align with your financial goals. This might involve allocating a specific budget for unplanned expenses or implementing a rule that involves waiting a certain period before making spontaneous decisions.

13.5 Incorporating Spontaneity into the Budget

To harmonize spontaneity and fiscal responsibility, integrate room for the unexpected into your budget. Designate a portion of your budget for discretionary spending, allowing flexibility for unplanned experiences or purchases. This proactive approach ensures that spontaneity remains a joyful aspect of life without jeopardizing long-term financial stability.

13.6 Evaluating Value and Impact

Before succumbing to the allure of a spontaneous purchase, evaluate its value and impact on your life. Ask yourself whether the item or experience aligns with your values and brings genuine joy. This reflective pause introduces a conscious element to the impulse purchasing paradox, enabling you to make decisions that contribute positively to your well-being.

13.7 Prioritizing Financial Goals

Maintaining financial responsibility involves a commitment to prioritizing long-term financial goals over momentary pleasures. Reflect on your overarching financial objectives, such as saving for a home, investing for the future, or achieving debt reduction. Keeping these goals in mind provides perspective and encourages you to make choices aligned with your broader financial strategy.

13.8 Embracing Mindful Consumption Practices

Adopting mindful consumption practices is pivotal in navigating the impulse purchasing paradox. Engage in intentional decision-making, be present in the moment, and cultivate an awareness of the emotional and financial dimensions of your choices. Mindful consumption empowers you to savor the joys of spontaneity while maintaining fiscal responsibility.

13.9 Learning from Experience

The impulse purchasing paradox is a dynamic interplay between spontaneity and financial responsibility, and learning from experience is an ongoing process. Reflect on past spontaneous purchases, both positive and regrettable, and use these experiences as lessons for future decision-making. Continuous learning contributes to the refinement of your approach to balancing the paradox.

13.10 Fostering a Holistic Approach to Life

Achieving harmony in the impulse purchasing paradox involves fostering a holistic approach to life. Embrace spontaneity as a source of joy and vitality, recognizing that the value of experiences often transcends material possessions. Cultivate a mindful and intentional lifestyle that balances the pleasures of the moment with a sustainable and responsible financial outlook.

Balancing spontaneity and fiscal responsibility is an art that requires conscious effort and self-awareness. By navigating the impulse purchasing paradox with intentionality, setting boundaries, and incorporating the lessons learned from both joys and regrets, you can create a harmonious relationship between the unexpected joys of life and the financial stability that underpins long-term well-being.

CHAPTER 14

PERSONAL FINANCE AND IMPULSE CONTROL

Budgeting in the Face of Temptation

Personal finance is a delicate dance between income, expenditures, and the ever-present temptation of impulsive purchases. In this chapter, we explore the critical role of impulse control in the realm of personal finance, offering strategies for effective budgeting that withstands the allure of spontaneous spending.

14.1 The Foundations of Financial Stability

At the core of sound personal finance lies the establishment of strong foundations. Begin by defining clear financial goals—whether it's building an emergency fund, saving for a home, or planning for retirement. These goals serve as beacons, guiding your financial decisions and instilling a sense of purpose that fortifies your resistance to impulsive temptations.

14.2 Crafting a Comprehensive Budget

A comprehensive budget is the cornerstone of effective personal finance. Detail your sources of income and categorize your expenditures, distinguishing between fixed and variable costs. Assign specific allocations for necessities, savings, and discretionary spending. This structured approach empowers you to make informed and intentional choices within the framework of your financial plan.

14.3 Allocating a Discretionary Spending Allowance

Recognizing the inevitability of discretionary spending, allocate a specific portion of your budget to accommodate spontaneous purchases. This discretionary spending allowance provides room for flexibility and enjoyment without jeopardizing the stability of your overall financial plan. It's a proactive strategy that acknowledges the need for balance between discipline and enjoyment.

14.4 Setting Realistic and Attainable Goals

Effective budgeting requires setting realistic and attainable financial goals. Establishing goals that are challenging yet achievable fosters a sense of accomplishment and motivation. This positive reinforcement contributes to impulse control, as the pursuit of your financial objectives becomes a gratifying journey rather than a restrictive imposition.

14.5 Embracing the Envelope System

The envelope system is a tangible and visual method to control discretionary spending. Allocate cash into envelopes designated for specific categories such as entertainment, dining out, or shopping. Once an envelope is empty, it serves as a natural limit, signaling that further spending in that category is not advisable. This hands-on approach enhances awareness and promotes disciplined choices.

14.6 Utilizing Technology for Tracking

In the digital age, technology provides a wealth of tools to aid in budgeting and tracking expenses. Mobile apps and online platforms offer real-time insights into your financial status, expenditures, and progress toward goals. Leveraging technology not only streamlines the budgeting process but also enhances your ability to resist impulsive purchases through informed decision-making.

14.7 Establishing Emergency Funds as Safety Nets

Emergency funds serve as crucial safety nets in the face of unexpected expenses or financial challenges. Allocate a portion of your budget to build and maintain an emergency fund. Knowing that you have a financial cushion in place reduces the urgency to resort to impulsive decisions during times of unforeseen circumstances.

14.8 Practicing Delayed Gratification

Delayed gratification is a potent strategy for bolstering impulse control. When confronted with the desire for a spontaneous purchase, practice delaying the decision. Give yourself time to consider the long-term impact, evaluate alternatives, and assess whether the item is a genuine necessity. This intentional delay fosters mindfulness and mitigates impulsive tendencies.

14.9 Seeking Accountability Partnerships

Enlist the support of friends, family members, or financial mentors to serve as accountability partners. Share your financial goals and budgeting strategies with them. Having someone to provide encouragement, guidance, and a gentle reminder of your financial priorities strengthens your resolve against impulsive temptations.

14.10 Regularly Reviewing and Adjusting Your Budget

Personal finance is a dynamic endeavor that requires periodic reviews and adjustments. Regularly revisit your budget to assess its alignment with your evolving financial circumstances and goals. Adjust categories, reallocate funds, and refine your budgeting strategies as needed. This iterative process ensures that your budget remains a resilient tool in the face of changing temptations and priorities.

In the pursuit of financial stability, impulse control is a linchpin. By crafting a comprehensive budget, setting realistic goals, and embracing disciplined strategies, you not only fortify your financial foundations but also create a framework that allows for the joys of life without succumbing to the pitfalls of impulsive spending. Remember, effective budgeting is a journey, and each intentional step contributes to a more secure and empowered financial future.

CHAPTER 15

COGNITIVE BIASES AND IMPULSE PURCHASING

How Our Minds Betray Us

The human mind, while remarkable in its complexity, is susceptible to a myriad of cognitive biases that can lead us astray, especially in the realm of impulse purchasing. In this chapter, we delve into the fascinating world of cognitive biases, exploring how these mental shortcuts and perceptual distortions play a pivotal role in driving impulsive decisions.

15.1 Understanding Cognitive Biases

Cognitive biases are inherent tendencies in human thinking that can systematically deviate from rational judgment. These biases, often a result of mental shortcuts or heuristics, influence the way we perceive information, make decisions, and interpret the world around us. In the context of impulse purchasing, several cognitive biases come into play, contributing to the allure and pitfalls of spontaneous buying.

15.2 Anchoring Bias and Perceived Value

Anchoring bias occurs when individuals rely too heavily on the first piece of information encountered when making decisions. In the context of shopping, the initial price presented, whether it's a discounted rate or a premium offering, acts as an anchor that influences subsequent perceptions of value. Retailers strategically use anchoring to manipulate perceptions and induce impulsive purchases.

15.3 Loss Aversion and Fear of Missing Out (FOMO)

Loss aversion is the tendency to prefer avoiding losses over acquiring equivalent gains. In the context of impulse purchasing, this bias can manifest as a fear of missing out (FOMO). The prospect of losing out on a limited-time offer or exclusive deal can trigger impulsive decisions, as individuals strive to avoid the perceived loss associated with not participating.

15.4 The Scarcity Effect and Urgency

The scarcity effect is a cognitive bias that places higher value on items perceived as scarce or in limited supply. Retailers leverage this bias by creating a sense of urgency, emphasizing limited quantities or time-sensitive offers. The fear of missing out on a rare opportunity intensifies the desire to make impulsive purchases before the perceived scarcity disappears.

15.5 Confirmation Bias and Justification

Confirmation bias involves seeking and favoring information that confirms one's preexisting beliefs or decisions. In the context of impulse buying, individuals may selectively focus on positive aspects of a product or selectively interpret information that supports the decision to make a spontaneous purchase. This bias contributes to post-purchase justification and minimizes cognitive dissonance.

15.6 Halo Effect and Emotional Associations

The halo effect is a cognitive bias where our overall impression of a person, brand, or product influences our evaluation of specific attributes. In the realm of impulse purchasing, positive emotional associations with a brand or product can create a halo effect, blurring objective judgment. Emotional connections can lead to impulsive decisions based on overall positive perceptions rather than a rational assessment of the specific purchase.

15.7 Present Bias and Immediate Gratification

Present bias involves giving more weight to immediate rewards at the expense of long-term benefits. This bias contributes significantly to impulse purchasing, as individuals prioritize the immediate gratification derived from acquiring a desired item over the potential long-term consequences on their finances. Retailers capitalize on present bias by emphasizing instant rewards and instant access to products.

15.8 Choice Overload and Decision Fatigue

Choice overload occurs when individuals are presented with too many options, leading to decision fatigue. In the context of shopping, a plethora of choices can overwhelm consumers, making them more susceptible to impulsive decisions as a coping mechanism to simplify the decision-making process. Retail environments that offer a wide array of products exploit this cognitive bias.

15.9 Social Proof and Conformity Bias

Social proof is the tendency to rely on the behavior and opinions of others as a guide for our own decisions. Conformity bias, or the desire to align with societal norms, plays a role in impulse purchasing as individuals are influenced by the buying behaviors of their peers or influencers. The collective endorsement of a product or trend becomes a powerful motivator for impulsive decisions.

15.10 Overcoming Cognitive Biases Through Awareness

Awareness is a potent tool in mitigating the impact of cognitive biases on impulse purchasing. Recognizing the existence of these biases and their potential influence on decision-making empowers individuals to approach shopping with a more critical and intentional mindset. By cultivating awareness, consumers can navigate the intricate landscape of cognitive biases, make more informed choices, and resist the subtle manipulations employed by marketers and retailers.

Understanding the cognitive biases that contribute to impulse purchasing is a key step in developing resilience against the allure of spontaneous buying. By acknowledging the intricate workings of our minds and cultivating awareness, individuals can reclaim control over their decision-making processes, making choices that align with their values and long-term financial well-being.

CHAPTER 16

BREAKING THE HABIT LOOP

Overcoming the Urge to Splurge

Impulse purchasing often stems from habitual behaviors ingrained in our daily lives. Breaking the habit loop requires a conscious effort to identify, understand, and reshape the patterns that drive impulsive decisions. In this chapter, we explore strategies for overcoming the urge to splurge and disrupting the habit loop associated with impulsive buying.

16.1 Recognizing the Triggers

The first step in breaking the habit loop is recognizing the triggers that initiate impulsive behaviors. Pay close attention to the situations, emotions, or environmental cues that precede spontaneous purchases. Whether it's stress, boredom, or a specific shopping environment, identifying these triggers is essential to understanding the root causes of the habit loop.

16.2 Mapping the Routine

Once the triggers are identified, map out the routine that follows. The routine is the series of actions and decisions that unfold after the trigger and lead to impulsive buying. It may involve entering a store, browsing online, or engaging in specific thought patterns. By visualizing the routine, individuals gain insight into the sequence of events that perpetuate the habit loop.

16.3 Analyzing the Reward System

The third component of the habit loop is the reward—the positive reinforcement that reinforces the impulsive behavior. Ask yourself what gratification or satisfaction the impulsive purchase provides. It could be a momentary thrill, a sense of accomplishment, or a distraction from negative emotions. Understanding the reward system is crucial for breaking the habit loop.

16.4 Introducing Alternative Rewards

Once the reward system is identified, explore alternative rewards that fulfill the same underlying needs without resorting to impulsive buying. If stress relief is the goal, consider incorporating activities like meditation, exercise, or spending time in nature. Experiment with healthier, non-consumerist alternatives that align with your values and contribute positively to your well-being.

16.5 Disrupting the Routine

Disrupting the routine is a key strategy for breaking the habit loop. Introduce intentional changes that interrupt the sequence of events leading to impulsive purchasing. This might involve altering your route to avoid passing by tempting stores, unsubscribing from promotional emails, or establishing a new pre-shopping ritual that reduces the likelihood of impulsive decisions.

16.6 Implementing a Delayed Gratification Technique

Introduce a delayed gratification technique to create a buffer between the trigger and the impulsive behavior. Set a predetermined waiting period before making a purchase, allowing time for emotions to settle and rational thinking to prevail. This intentional delay disrupts the immediacy of the habit loop and provides an opportunity to reevaluate the decision.

16.7 Engaging in Mindfulness Practices

Mindfulness practices, such as meditation and mindful breathing, cultivate awareness and presence in the moment. Incorporate mindfulness into your daily routine to become more attuned to your thoughts, emotions, and the impulse to splurge. Mindfulness enhances self-regulation and empowers individuals to make more conscious choices, disrupting the habit loop.

16.8 Establishing a Support System

Breaking the habit loop is a challenging journey that benefits from a support system. Share your goal of overcoming impulsive buying habits with friends, family, or a mentor. Having a support network provides encouragement, accountability, and a source of guidance during moments of temptation. Celebrate successes together and learn from setbacks as a collective effort.

16.9 Tracking Progress and Celebrating Milestones

Keep track of your progress in breaking the habit loop. Establish milestones and celebrate achievements along the way. Whether it's a week without impulsive purchases or successfully resisting a specific trigger, acknowledging progress reinforces positive behaviors and motivates continued efforts to overcome the urge to splurge.

16.10 Seeking Professional Guidance if Needed

For individuals facing persistent challenges in breaking the habit loop, seeking professional guidance can be beneficial. Behavioral therapists, psychologists, or financial counselors specializing in impulsive behaviors can provide tailored strategies and support. Professional guidance offers a structured and personalized approach to breaking ingrained habits and fostering healthier decision-making.

Breaking the habit loop associated with impulse purchasing requires dedication, self-awareness, and a commitment to change. By recognizing triggers, analyzing routines, and introducing intentional disruptions, individuals can reshape their behaviors and overcome the urge to splurge. The journey to breaking the habit loop is a transformative process that leads to greater control over spending habits and a more intentional and mindful approach to consumption.

CHAPTER 17

IMPULSE BUYING IN DIFFERENT CULTURES

Cross-Cultural Perspectives

Impulse buying is a phenomenon that manifests differently across various cultures, shaped by societal norms, values, and consumer behaviors unique to each cultural context. In this chapter, we explore the cross-cultural perspectives of impulse buying, shedding light on the factors that influence impulsive behaviors and the nuanced ways in which different cultures navigate the allure of spontaneous purchasing.

17.1 Cultural Influences on Consumer Behavior

Culture plays a pivotal role in shaping consumer behavior, influencing perceptions of needs, desires, and the value attached to material possessions. Cultural dimensions such as individualism, collectivism, power distance, and uncertainty avoidance contribute to variations in how impulse buying is expressed and perceived across different cultures.

17.2 Collectivism and Group Dynamics

In cultures that emphasize collectivism, such as many Asian societies, group dynamics significantly impact impulse buying. Decisions may be influenced by the preferences and opinions of family, friends, or social groups. The desire to conform to group norms and maintain social harmony can either amplify or mitigate impulsive tendencies, depending on cultural values.

17.3 Individualism and Self-Expression

Conversely, cultures that prioritize individualism, such as many Western societies, often see impulse buying as a means of expressing personal identity and fulfilling individual desires. The emphasis on autonomy and self-expression can lead to a heightened pursuit of spontaneous purchases driven by the desire for uniqueness and personal gratification.

17.4 Power Distance and Authority Influence

Power distance, or the extent to which a culture accepts hierarchical authority, can impact impulsive buying. In cultures with high power distance, individuals may be more susceptible to the influence of authority figures, such as celebrities or influencers, leading to impulsive decisions influenced by external endorsements. In contrast, cultures with lower power distance may exhibit greater individual autonomy in purchasing decisions.

17.5 Cultural Attitudes Toward Time

Cultural attitudes toward time also play a role in impulse buying. Some cultures, particularly those with a polychronic orientation, may place less emphasis on strict schedules and deadlines. In such contexts, spontaneous purchases may be more readily integrated into daily life, driven by a flexible and less time-bound approach to activities.

17.6 Rituals and Celebratory Buying

Cultural rituals and celebrations often provide occasions for impulse buying. Festivals, holidays, and special events may trigger an increased willingness to make spontaneous purchases as individuals seek to partake in cultural traditions, express generosity, or enhance the celebratory atmosphere through impulsive buying.

17.7 Cultural Perceptions of Luxury and Status

Cultural perspectives on luxury and status influence impulsive buying behaviors. In some cultures, the acquisition of luxury items is seen as a symbol of social status and success, driving impulsive decisions to align with societal expectations. In contrast, cultures with different values may prioritize frugality or place less emphasis on material possessions, influencing the prevalence and nature of impulse buying.

17.8 Marketing and Cultural Sensitivity

Successful marketing strategies in cross-cultural contexts require cultural sensitivity. Advertisers must understand the nuances of cultural values, preferences, and buying behaviors to effectively appeal to diverse audiences. Cultural symbols, language nuances, and the portrayal of social norms play critical roles in shaping the effectiveness of marketing campaigns targeting impulsive buying tendencies.

17.9 Globalization and Cultural Homogenization

As globalization advances, cultural boundaries blur, and consumer behaviors become more interconnected. While globalization can lead to the diffusion of impulsive buying tendencies across cultures, it also fosters the adaptation and integration of cultural influences. The intersection of global and local factors creates a dynamic landscape where cross-cultural perspectives on impulse buying continually evolve.

17.10 Cultural Adaptation and Impulse Control Strategies

Individuals navigating diverse cultural contexts may develop cultural adaptation and impulse control strategies. This may involve adjusting to local norms, understanding cultural triggers, and adopting behaviors that align with cultural expectations. Cross-cultural competence in managing impulsive tendencies is an essential skill for individuals operating in globalized environments.

Understanding impulse buying through cross-cultural perspectives enhances our appreciation of the intricate interplay between cultural factors and consumer behaviors. By recognizing the diverse ways in which impulse buying manifests across cultures, individuals, marketers, and policymakers can cultivate cultural intelligence, promote cultural sensitivity, and tailor strategies that align with the unique dynamics of each cultural context.

CHAPTER 18

PEER PRESSURE AND IMPULSE PURCHASES

Navigating the Social Influence

Peer pressure, a powerful force in social dynamics, can significantly impact consumer behavior, particularly in the realm of impulse purchases. In this chapter, we explore the intricate relationship between peer pressure and impulsive buying, examining the mechanisms through which social influence shapes individual decisions and offering strategies to navigate the allure of spontaneous purchases in social settings.

18.1 The Social Dynamics of Peer Pressure

Peer pressure refers to the influence exerted by one's social group to conform to certain behaviors, attitudes, or decisions. In the context of consumerism, peer pressure can lead individuals to make impulsive purchases influenced by the desire to fit in, gain social approval, or avoid social exclusion. Understanding the social dynamics at play is essential for navigating the impact of peer pressure on impulsive buying.

18.2 Social Norms and Conformity

Social norms, the unwritten rules governing acceptable behavior within a group, significantly influence impulse buying. The desire to conform to these norms can lead individuals to make spontaneous purchases to align with the perceived expectations of their peers. Conformity becomes a powerful motivator, as individuals strive to maintain social harmony and acceptance within their social circles.

18.3 The Fear of Missing Out (FOMO)

The Fear of Missing Out (FOMO) is a potent aspect of peer pressure that drives impulsive purchasing. Individuals experiencing FOMO may succumb to the pressure of joining in on group activities or acquiring trending products to avoid the perceived loss of exclusion. The urgency associated with FOMO intensifies the impulse to make quick and spontaneous buying decisions.

18.4 Peer Influence on Product Choices

Peers play a pivotal role in shaping product choices and preferences. Recommendations, endorsements, and shared experiences within a social group can significantly impact the decision-making process. The desire to emulate the choices of admired peers or to share common interests can lead to impulsive purchases driven by the need to align with the group's preferences.

18.5 Social Comparison and Status Symbolism

Social comparison, the act of evaluating oneself in relation to others, contributes to impulsive buying as individuals seek to match or surpass the possessions of their peers. The pursuit of status symbolism through material acquisitions becomes a driving force, with impulsive purchases serving as a means of signaling one's social standing within the peer group.

18.6 Peer Pressure in Physical and Digital Spaces

Peer pressure extends beyond physical interactions to digital spaces, where social media platforms amplify its impact. The curated displays of lifestyles, possessions, and experiences on social media create a virtual environment where individuals feel compelled to keep up with the perceived standards set by their online peers. Digital peer pressure can trigger impulsive buying in the pursuit of online validation and social recognition.

18.7 Strategies for Navigating Peer Pressure

Navigating peer pressure requires a combination of self-awareness and strategic approaches:

18.7.1 Cultivate Individual Values: Develop a strong sense of individual values and priorities. Understanding what truly matters to you provides a foundation for making purchasing decisions aligned with your personal goals, irrespective of external influences.

18.7.2 Set Clear Spending Boundaries: Establish clear boundaries for discretionary spending. Define limits that align with your financial goals and values, and communicate these boundaries to your peers. Having predefined spending limits helps resist impulsive purchases pushed by external pressures.

18.7.3 Be Selective in Social Circles: Surround yourself with individuals who respect your financial goals and values. Selective social circles that prioritize shared values reduce the likelihood of succumbing to negative peer pressure and encourage positive and supportive influences.

18.7.4 Practice Assertiveness: Develop assertiveness skills to express your preferences and resist external pressures. Politely decline invitations or suggestions that conflict with your financial priorities. Communicate assertively without compromising your individual goals.

18.7.5 Utilize Peer Support: Leverage peer support as a positive influence. Share your financial goals with friends who understand and support your aspirations. Mutual encouragement within the peer group can foster a collective commitment to responsible spending.

18.7.6 Embrace Responsible Role Modeling: Be a responsible role model within your social circle. Demonstrate intentional and mindful consumption, emphasizing the importance of thoughtful decision-making over impulsive actions. Your example can positively influence others.

18.7.7 Digital Detox: Periodically disconnect from social media to reduce the influence of digital peer pressure. Taking breaks from online platforms allows for greater clarity, minimizing the impact of curated content on impulsive buying decisions.

18.7.8 Reflect on Long-Term Goals: Regularly reflect on your long-term financial goals. Consider the impact of impulsive purchases on your overall financial well-being and aspirations. Keeping sight of your broader objectives provides motivation to resist short-term pressures.

Navigating the influence of peer pressure on impulse purchases involves a combination of self-awareness, assertiveness, and strategic decision-making. By cultivating a strong sense of individual values, setting clear boundaries, and surrounding yourself with a supportive social network, you can navigate the complex dynamics of peer pressure and make purchasing decisions aligned with your financial priorities.

CHAPTER 19

RETAIL THERAPY OR RETAIL TRAP?

Understanding the Thin Line

The concept of retail therapy, the practice of shopping to improve one's mood or alleviate stress, is deeply ingrained in contemporary culture. However, the fine line between retail therapy as a source of comfort and the retail trap that ensnares individuals in impulsive buying patterns is a nuanced and often precarious distinction. In this chapter, we explore the dynamics of retail therapy, its psychological underpinnings, and the potential pitfalls that transform it into a retail trap.

19.1 The Psychology of Retail Therapy

Retail therapy is rooted in the idea that shopping can provide a temporary escape from negative emotions or stress. The act of making a purchase, whether small or significant, triggers a release of dopamine—the "feel-good" neurotransmitter—which contributes to a sense of reward and pleasure. Understanding the psychological mechanisms behind retail therapy is crucial for discerning its therapeutic aspects from potential pitfalls.

19.2 The Comfort of Consumption

For many, retail therapy serves as a coping mechanism, offering a sense of control, comfort, and distraction during challenging times. The act of acquiring new possessions provides a tangible and immediate source of gratification, momentarily alleviating stress and creating a positive emotional response. The comfort derived from consumption is a central aspect of retail therapy.

19.3 Emotional Triggers and Impulse Buying

While retail therapy can be a legitimate means of self-care, it becomes a retail trap when emotional triggers consistently lead to impulsive buying. Emotional states such as sadness, boredom, or anxiety may act as catalysts, prompting individuals to seek solace through shopping without a thoughtful consideration of the long-term consequences.

19.4 The Retail Trap: Uncontrolled Consumption

The retail trap emerges when the act of shopping transitions from a conscious and intentional practice to uncontrolled and compulsive consumption. Individuals caught in the retail trap may find themselves making impulsive purchases without genuine need or consideration of their financial well-being. The temporary relief provided by retail therapy transforms into a cycle of excessive and potentially harmful spending.

19.5 Recognizing Warning Signs

To differentiate between retail therapy and the retail trap, it's essential to recognize warning signs that indicate a shift towards uncontrolled consumption. These signs may include:

- **Frequent Impulse Purchases:** Consistent, unplanned buying without a clear need or purpose.

- **Financial Strain:** Experiencing financial difficulties or accumulating debt due to impulsive spending.

- **Emotional Dependency:** Relying heavily on shopping as the primary means of managing emotions.

- **Post-Purchase Regret:** Experiencing remorse or guilt after impulsive purchases.

- **Lack of Budgetary Awareness:** Ignoring budgetary constraints and spending beyond one's means.

19.6 Strategies for Healthy Retail Therapy

To ensure that retail therapy remains a source of comfort rather than a retail trap, consider implementing the following strategies:

- **Mindful Consumption:** Practice mindful shopping by being aware of your emotions, intentions, and the impact of purchases on your well-being.

- **Establishing Boundaries:** Set clear boundaries for retail therapy spending to prevent excessive and impulsive purchases.

- **Alternatives to Consumption:** Explore non-consumerist alternatives such as engaging in hobbies, physical activities, or social interactions as means of emotional support.

- **Building Emotional Resilience:** Develop coping mechanisms beyond shopping to build emotional resilience and address stressors in a healthier manner.

- **Periodic Reflection:** Regularly reflect on your shopping habits, evaluating whether they align with your values and long-term goals.

19.7 Seeking Professional Guidance

For individuals struggling to navigate the thin line between retail therapy and the retail trap, seeking professional guidance can be instrumental. Financial counselors, therapists, or support groups specializing in consumer behavior can offer insights, strategies, and a structured approach to overcoming impulsive buying patterns.

19.8 Cultivating a Balanced Approach

Ultimately, the key to harnessing the therapeutic aspects of retail therapy while avoiding the pitfalls of the retail trap lies in cultivating a balanced and intentional approach to consumption. By maintaining self-awareness, setting boundaries, and seeking support when needed, individuals can navigate the thin line between retail therapy and the retail trap, ensuring that shopping remains a positive and mindful activity within the broader context of their lives.

CHAPTER 20

THE IMPULSE PURCHASE DIARY

A Tool for Self-Reflection

In the quest for understanding and mastering impulse purchasing behaviors, the Impulse Purchase Diary emerges as a valuable tool for self-reflection and awareness. This chapter introduces the concept of the Impulse Purchase Diary, explores its benefits, and provides guidance on how to effectively use this tool to gain insights into impulsive buying patterns and cultivate mindful consumption habits.

20.1 The Power of Reflection

Reflection is a potent catalyst for personal growth and behavioral change. The Impulse Purchase Diary harnesses the power of reflection to illuminate the factors contributing to impulsive purchases, fostering a deeper understanding of individual motivations, triggers, and emotions associated with spontaneous buying.

20.2 Components of the Impulse Purchase Diary

The Impulse Purchase Diary is a structured journal that encourages individuals to document their impulsive buying experiences systematically. The diary typically includes the following components:

20.2.1 Date and Time: Record the date and time of the impulsive purchase. This information provides context and helps identify patterns related to specific times of day or days of the week.

20.2.2 Location: Note where the impulsive purchase occurred, whether it was online, in a specific store, or during a particular activity. Location can unveil environmental triggers influencing impulsive decisions.

20.2.3 Item Purchased: Specify the item or service purchased impulsively. Include details such as brand, description, and cost. Documenting the specifics sheds light on preferences and trends in impulsive buying.

20.2.4 Emotional State: Reflect on your emotional state before and after the impulsive purchase. Identify the emotions driving the decision, whether it was stress, excitement, boredom, or other feelings.

20.2.5 Triggers: Identify the triggers that prompted the impulsive purchase. Triggers can encompass external influences, emotional states, or situational factors that instigated the buying decision.

20.2.6 Justification: Document any justifications or rationalizations made during or after the impulsive purchase. Analyzing justifications provides insights into the cognitive processes involved in impulsive buying.

20.2.7 Post-Purchase Feelings: Reflect on how you felt after making the impulsive purchase. Consider whether feelings of satisfaction, regret, or guilt emerged and the duration of these emotions.

20.3 Benefits of the Impulse Purchase Diary

The Impulse Purchase Diary offers several benefits that contribute to the development of mindful consumption habits:

20.3.1 Increased Self-Awareness: By consistently documenting impulsive purchases, individuals gain a heightened awareness of their buying patterns, triggers, and emotional responses.

20.3.2 Identification of Patterns: Over time, patterns and trends in impulsive buying become apparent, allowing individuals to identify recurring themes and address them proactively.

20.3.3 Targeted Intervention: Armed with insights from the diary, individuals can implement targeted interventions to address specific triggers, emotions, or circumstances that contribute to impulsive buying.

20.3.4 Informed Decision-Making: The Impulse Purchase Diary equips individuals with information to make more informed decisions about their spending habits, fostering a sense of control and intentionality.

20.3.5 Behavior Modification: The act of consistently reflecting on impulsive purchases creates a foundation for behavior modification, enabling individuals to gradually shift towards more mindful and intentional consumption.

20.4 How to Use the Impulse Purchase Diary Effectively

20.4.1 Consistency is Key: Establish a routine for diary entries. Consistent documentation provides a comprehensive view of impulsive buying behaviors over time.

20.4.2 Honest Self-Reflection: Be honest and transparent in your reflections. Acknowledge both positive and negative emotions associated with impulsive purchases to facilitate meaningful self-reflection.

20.4.3 Regular Review: Set aside time for regular reviews of your diary entries. Analyze patterns, identify triggers, and reflect on your progress in cultivating mindful consumption habits.

20.4.4 Adjustments and Adaptations: As patterns emerge, be open to making adjustments and adaptations to your approach. Implement strategies to address specific triggers and experiment with alternative coping mechanisms.

20.4.5 Celebrate Progress: Celebrate achievements and progress in developing mindful consumption habits. Recognize and reward positive changes in behavior to reinforce a commitment to intentional spending.

20.5 Seeking Professional Guidance

For individuals facing persistent challenges in overcoming impulsive buying behaviors, seeking professional guidance can provide additional support. Financial counselors, psychologists, or behavioral therapists can offer personalized strategies and insights to address underlying factors contributing to impulsive purchases.

20.6 Closing Thoughts

The Impulse Purchase Diary serves as a transformative tool in the journey towards mindful consumption. By embracing the power of reflection, consistently documenting impulsive purchases, and leveraging the insights gained, individuals can navigate the path from impulsive buying to intentional, conscious, and fulfilling consumption. The diary becomes a companion on this journey, fostering self-awareness, empowering informed decision-making,

CHAPTER 21

THE ETHICAL DIMENSIONS OF IMPULSE SELLING

Balancing Profit and Responsibility

In the dynamic landscape of commerce, the ethical dimensions of impulse selling emerge as a critical consideration. As businesses strive to maximize profits, the fine line between encouraging consumer engagement and responsible selling practices becomes increasingly significant. This chapter delves into the ethical dimensions of impulse selling, exploring the impact on consumers, businesses, and the broader societal landscape, while emphasizing the need to strike a delicate balance between profit motives and ethical responsibility.

21.1 The Power and Responsibility of Sellers

Sellers wield significant influence over consumer behavior, especially in the realm of impulse selling. The power to shape purchasing decisions comes with a concomitant responsibility to prioritize consumer well-being, transparency, and ethical conduct. As businesses pursue profits, ethical considerations must remain at the forefront of their strategies.

21.2 Transparency in Marketing Practices

Transparency is a cornerstone of ethical impulse selling. Businesses are obligated to provide accurate information about products, pricing, and promotions. Ambiguity or misleading tactics erode consumer trust and contribute to impulsive purchases driven by misinformation.

21.3 Balancing Persuasion and Coercion

The line between persuasive marketing and coercion is a delicate one. Ethical impulse selling relies on persuasive techniques that inform and engage consumers without unduly pressuring or manipulating them. Striking this balance safeguards consumers from making purchases against their better judgment.

21.4 The Impact on Vulnerable Consumer Groups

Vulnerable consumer groups, such as children, individuals with limited financial literacy, and those susceptible to compulsive behaviors, require heightened ethical considerations. Businesses must exercise caution in targeting these groups to prevent exploitation and ensure that impulse selling practices do not disproportionately impact vulnerable individuals.

21.5 Environmental Considerations

Ethical impulse selling extends beyond individual consumers to encompass broader societal impacts. Businesses must assess the environmental consequences of their marketing strategies, particularly the promotion of disposable or unnecessary products. A commitment to sustainability and eco-friendly practices aligns with ethical responsibility.

21.6 Addressing Behavioral Addictions

Impulse selling can inadvertently contribute to behavioral addictions, where individuals develop compulsive buying habits. Businesses should actively address the ethical implications of fostering addictive behaviors and take steps to minimize harm, such as providing resources for responsible consumption and addiction support.

21.7 Social Responsibility in Marketing

Social responsibility is integral to ethical impulse selling. Businesses can actively contribute to the well-being of society by aligning marketing efforts with social causes, promoting ethical sourcing practices, and engaging in philanthropic initiatives. Consumers increasingly value businesses that demonstrate a commitment to social responsibility.

21.8 Ethical Considerations in E-Commerce

In the age of e-commerce, ethical considerations in impulse selling extend to digital platforms. Businesses operating online must prioritize data privacy, secure transactions, and transparent communication to uphold ethical standards and protect consumers in the digital space.

21.9 Regulatory Compliance

Governments and regulatory bodies play a crucial role in shaping the ethical landscape of impulse selling. Enforcing and updating regulations that protect consumers from unethical marketing practices, including deceptive advertising and hidden fees, is essential for maintaining a fair marketplace.

21.10 Striking a Balance: Profit and Responsibility

Striking a balance between profit motives and ethical responsibility is a complex yet essential endeavor. Businesses can pursue profitability while adhering to ethical principles by:

- **Implementing Transparent Practices:** Communicate openly with consumers about products, pricing, and promotional strategies to foster trust.

- **Prioritizing Consumer Well-Being:** Consider the potential impact of marketing strategies on consumer well-being and mental health, avoiding tactics that exploit vulnerabilities.

- **Investing in Ethical Marketing Training:** Provide employees with training on ethical marketing practices, emphasizing the importance of responsible selling.

- **Collaborating with Ethical Standards Organizations:** Engage with and adhere to ethical standards established by industry organizations or consumer advocacy groups to demonstrate a commitment to responsible business practices.

- **Engaging in Stakeholder Dialogue:** Foster open dialogue with consumers, employees, and other stakeholders to understand concerns and incorporate ethical considerations into business strategies.

21.11 The Future of Ethical Impulse Selling

As consumer awareness of ethical considerations continues to grow, the future of impulse selling lies in businesses adapting to a more conscientious approach. Ethical impulse selling is not only a moral imperative but also a strategic advantage, as consumers increasingly gravitate toward businesses that prioritize responsibility, transparency, and the well-being of both individuals and the broader community.

21.12 Closing Reflections

The ethical dimensions of impulse selling underscore the need for a harmonious relationship between businesses and consumers. By navigating the intricate balance between profit and responsibility, businesses can contribute to a marketplace that values transparency, respects individual autonomy, and fosters ethical considerations in every impulse-driven transaction.

CHAPTER 22

MARKETING TO THE MINDFUL CONSUMER

Shifting Trends in Consumer Behavior

In an era marked by heightened awareness of sustainability, ethical practices, and mindful living, businesses must adapt their marketing strategies to resonate with the mindful consumer. This chapter explores the shifting trends in consumer behavior, delving into the characteristics of mindful consumers, and providing insights into effective marketing approaches that align with the values and priorities of this discerning and conscious demographic.

22.1 The Rise of the Mindful Consumer

The mindful consumer represents a paradigm shift in the marketplace—a demographic characterized by a heightened consciousness of the environmental, social, and ethical implications of their purchasing decisions. This shift is driven by a desire for transparency, sustainability, and a commitment to making choices that align with personal values.

22.2 Characteristics of the Mindful Consumer

Understanding the characteristics of the mindful consumer is crucial for businesses seeking to connect with this evolving demographic:

22.2.1 Sustainability Awareness: Mindful consumers prioritize sustainable practices, seeking products and services that minimize environmental impact and promote eco-friendly initiatives.

22.2.2 Ethical Sourcing: The mindful consumer values ethical sourcing, demanding transparency in the supply chain and supporting businesses that prioritize fair labor practices.

22.2.3 Social Responsibility: Socially responsible initiatives resonate with mindful consumers. Businesses engaged in philanthropy, community engagement, and social causes attract the attention and loyalty of this demographic.

22.2.4 Value Alignment: Mindful consumers seek value alignment with the brands they support. They are more likely to choose products and services that align with their personal values and beliefs.

22.2.5 Quality Over Quantity: The focus on mindful living extends to a preference for quality over quantity. Mindful consumers are willing to invest in well-crafted, durable products that stand the test of time.

22.2.6 Digital Savvy: Mindful consumers leverage digital platforms to research products, compare brands, and make informed decisions. An online presence that communicates transparency and authenticity is essential.

22.3 Adapting Marketing Strategies for Mindful Consumers

Businesses can tailor their marketing strategies to effectively resonate with mindful consumers by incorporating the following approaches:

22.3.1 Authentic Storytelling: Authenticity is paramount. Share transparent narratives about your brand's journey, values, and commitment to sustainability. Authentic storytelling fosters a genuine connection with mindful consumers.

22.3.2 Transparency in Communication: Provide clear and transparent information about product sourcing, manufacturing processes, and environmental impact. Mindful consumers appreciate openness and honesty in communication.

22.3.3 Emphasizing Sustainable Practices: Showcase your commitment to sustainability. Highlight eco-friendly practices, such as using recycled materials, reducing carbon footprint, and implementing environmentally conscious policies.

22.3.4 Social Responsibility Initiatives: Engage in meaningful social responsibility initiatives. Mindful consumers are drawn to businesses that actively contribute to social causes and demonstrate a commitment to making a positive impact.

22.3.5 Collaborations with Ethical Organizations: Partner with ethical organizations or obtain certifications that validate your commitment to responsible business practices. Affiliations with reputable ethical entities enhance credibility.

22.3.6 Mindful Packaging: Reevaluate packaging practices to minimize waste and environmental impact. Mindful consumers appreciate sustainable packaging solutions, such as biodegradable materials or minimalistic designs.

22.3.7 Digital Engagement and Education: Leverage digital platforms to engage with mindful consumers. Use social media, blogs, and other online channels to educate your audience about your brand's values, initiatives, and the ethical dimensions of your products.

22.3.8 Loyalty Programs with Purpose: Design loyalty programs that extend beyond discounts and promotions. Offer rewards that align with mindful consumers' values, such as contributions to charitable causes or exclusive access to sustainable products.

22.4 The Future of Mindful Consumerism

As the mindful consumer demographic continues to grow, the future of consumerism is shaped by a collective consciousness towards responsible choices. Businesses that proactively embrace and adapt to this shift will not only meet the evolving demands of consumers but also contribute to a more sustainable and ethical marketplace.

22.5 Closing Thoughts

Marketing to the mindful consumer requires a holistic approach that transcends traditional advertising. By authentically aligning with the values of mindful consumers, businesses can forge lasting connections, foster brand loyalty, and contribute to a marketplace where ethical considerations and sustainability are at the forefront of consumer decision-making. As the landscape of consumer behavior evolves, the businesses that prioritize mindfulness and responsibility will thrive in this new era of conscious commerce.

CHAPTER 23

THE ROLE OF TECHNOLOGY IN IMPULSE PURCHASING

From Augmented Reality to Virtual Carts

In the ever-evolving landscape of commerce, technology plays a pivotal role in shaping consumer behaviors, particularly in the realm of impulse purchasing. This chapter explores the multifaceted influence of technology on impulse buying, examining how innovations such as augmented reality (AR), virtual reality (VR), and virtual shopping carts have transformed the consumer experience and the dynamics of impulsive decision-making.

23.1 The Digital Transformation of Commerce

The integration of technology into commerce has ushered in a new era of consumer engagement. As digital platforms become integral to the shopping experience, businesses leverage innovative technologies to capture attention, enhance interactivity, and prompt impulsive purchases.

23.2 Augmented Reality (AR) in Retail

Augmented reality overlays digital information onto the physical world, creating immersive and interactive experiences. In retail, AR enables consumers to visualize products in real-world environments before making a purchase. This visualization aspect significantly influences impulsive buying, as consumers can assess how a product fits into their lives, fostering a sense of immediacy and connection.

23.3 Virtual Reality (VR) Shopping Experiences

Virtual reality elevates the shopping experience by transporting consumers to virtual environments. VR shopping allows users to explore products in three-dimensional spaces, providing a heightened sense of presence and engagement. The immersive nature of VR can intensify impulsive buying tendencies, as consumers feel more connected to the products they virtually interact with.

23.4 Personalized Recommendations and Algorithms

Technology-driven algorithms analyze vast amounts of consumer data to deliver personalized product recommendations. These recommendations, tailored to individual preferences and behavior patterns, create a sense of relevance and urgency, prompting impulsive purchases based on the perception of exclusivity or personalized value.

23.5 Social Media Integration

Social media platforms serve as dynamic spaces for impulse purchasing. The seamless integration of shopping features within social apps allows users to discover and buy products without leaving the platform. Influencer endorsements, visually appealing content, and limited-time promotions on social media contribute to the impulse-driven nature of purchases.

23.6 One-Click Purchases and Instant Checkout

Simplified checkout processes, exemplified by one-click purchases, remove friction from the buying journey. The immediacy of completing a purchase with a single click capitalizes on impulsive tendencies, reducing the time for consumers to reconsider their decisions and enhancing the convenience of impulse buying.

23.7 Virtual Shopping Carts and Abandoned Cart Strategies

Virtual shopping carts in e-commerce platforms facilitate the accumulation of items for future purchase. Businesses employ strategies to address abandoned carts, such as sending reminders or offering discounts, to rekindle interest and prompt impulsive purchases. The virtual cart becomes a tool for both consumer convenience and strategic marketing.

23.8 Gamification of Shopping

Gamification techniques, such as limited-time offers, flash sales, and reward systems, infuse an element of excitement into the shopping experience. By turning the act of shopping into a game, businesses capitalize on consumers' desire for novel and engaging experiences, heightening the allure of impulsive purchases.

23.9 Wearable Technology and Mobile Shopping Apps

Wearable devices and mobile shopping apps bring the convenience of impulse buying to users' fingertips. Notifications, alerts, and personalized offers delivered through wearables and apps create immediate opportunities for impulsive purchases, seamlessly integrating shopping into users' daily lives.

23.10 Ethical Considerations in Technologically Driven Impulse Buying

While technology enhances the efficiency and appeal of impulse buying, ethical considerations arise. Businesses must navigate the fine line between leveraging technology to enhance the consumer experience and ensuring responsible marketing practices that prioritize transparency, user consent, and data security.

23.11 Consumer Empowerment Through Technology

Technology not only shapes impulsive buying behaviors but also empowers consumers. Access to information, user reviews, and price comparisons enable consumers to make more informed decisions. As technology continues to advance, businesses that prioritize consumer empowerment and ethical considerations will build trust and loyalty.

23.12 The Future of Technology and Impulse Purchasing

The future of technology and impulse purchasing holds the promise of even more innovative and immersive experiences. Advancements in artificial intelligence, augmented reality, and virtual reality will likely redefine the boundaries of impulse buying, offering personalized and engaging interactions that cater to individual preferences.

23.13 Balancing Innovation and Responsibility

As businesses harness the power of technology to drive impulse purchasing, it is essential to strike a balance between innovation and responsibility. Ethical considerations, user privacy, and transparency should guide the integration of technology into the shopping experience, ensuring that technological advancements enhance consumer empowerment without compromising ethical standards.

23.14 Closing Thoughts

The role of technology in impulse purchasing is dynamic and ever-expanding. As businesses embrace technological innovations, they have the opportunity to create seamless, personalized, and ethical shopping experiences that align with the evolving expectations of modern consumers. The intersection of technology and impulse buying marks a compelling chapter in the ongoing narrative of commerce, offering both challenges and opportunities for businesses and consumers alike.

CHAPTER 24

EDUCATION AND IMPULSE CONTROL

Impulse Management as a Life Skill

In the realm of personal development and well-being, impulse control stands out as a fundamental life skill. This chapter explores the intersection between education and impulse control, recognizing the pivotal role that learning and self-awareness play in cultivating the ability to manage impulses effectively. By examining the impact of education on impulse control as a life skill, we uncover strategies and insights that empower individuals to make intentional choices and navigate the complexities of decision-making.

24.1 The Significance of Impulse Control

Impulse control, the ability to resist immediate desires and make thoughtful decisions, is a cornerstone of emotional intelligence and personal effectiveness. Education serves as a catalyst for developing and refining this essential life skill, providing individuals with the tools to make informed choices that align with their long-term goals and values.

24.2 The Educational Foundation of Impulse Control

Education, in its broadest sense, encompasses formal schooling, self-directed learning, and experiential knowledge gained throughout life. The educational foundation of impulse control includes:

24.2.1 Cognitive Awareness: Education instills cognitive awareness by fostering an understanding of the consequences of impulsive decisions. Individuals equipped with knowledge are better equipped to anticipate the outcomes of their actions, enabling them to make decisions aligned with their broader objectives.

24.2.2 Emotional Regulation: Educational settings offer opportunities to learn and practice emotional regulation, a key component of impulse control. By acquiring emotional intelligence through education, individuals can navigate challenging situations without succumbing to impulsive reactions driven by intense emotions.

24.2.3 Critical Thinking Skills: Education cultivates critical thinking skills, empowering individuals to evaluate situations, assess potential outcomes, and make rational decisions. The ability to analyze information critically contributes to effective impulse control.

24.2.4 Goal Setting and Planning: Goal-oriented education encourages individuals to set long-term objectives and create actionable plans. The process of goal setting and planning fosters a forward-looking perspective, mitigating the allure of immediate gratification in favor of sustained achievement.

24.2.5 Self-Reflection Practices: Education encourages self-reflection, providing individuals with the tools to examine their thoughts, behaviors, and motivations. Regular self-reflection enhances self-awareness, a crucial component of impulse control.

24.3 Strategies for Integrating Impulse Control into Education

To effectively integrate impulse control as a life skill into educational settings, educators and learners can implement the following strategies:

24.3.1 Mindfulness Practices: Incorporate mindfulness practices into educational curricula to enhance self-awareness and emotional regulation. Mindfulness techniques, such as meditation and deep breathing exercises, contribute to a centered and focused mindset.

24.3.2 Case Studies and Scenarios: Use real-life case studies and scenarios to explore the consequences of impulsive decisions. Engaging with practical examples enables learners to apply theoretical knowledge to tangible situations.

24.3.3 Role-Playing Exercises: Employ role-playing exercises that simulate decision-making scenarios. Role-playing provides a safe space for individuals to practice impulse control and explore alternative courses of action.

24.3.4 Incorporating Emotional Intelligence Education: Integrate emotional intelligence education into formal curricula. Develop programs that teach students to recognize, understand, and manage their emotions, fostering emotional resilience and impulse control.

24.3.5 Goal-Setting Workshops: Facilitate goal-setting workshops that guide individuals in articulating their long-term aspirations. Encourage participants to break down goals into actionable steps, promoting a strategic and intentional approach to decision-making.

24.3.6 Collaborative Learning Environments: Foster collaborative learning environments that encourage open dialogue and the exchange of perspectives. Interacting with diverse viewpoints enhances critical thinking skills and broadens individuals' understanding of the consequences of impulsive choices.

24.3.7 Mentorship Programs: Implement mentorship programs that pair individuals with experienced mentors. Mentors can provide guidance on impulse control based on their own experiences, offering valuable insights and strategies for making intentional decisions.

24.4 Lifelong Learning and Continued Development

Impulse control is not a static skill but a dynamic aspect of personal development that evolves over time. Lifelong learning, characterized by a commitment to ongoing education and self-improvement, ensures that individuals continue to refine their impulse management skills throughout various stages of life.

24.5 The Impact of Impulse Control on Academic and Professional Success

Education and impulse control are intertwined elements that significantly impact academic and professional success. Individuals with strong impulse control are better equipped to navigate academic challenges, make strategic career decisions, and foster positive relationships in professional settings. The ability to delay gratification and make thoughtful choices enhances one's overall effectiveness and resilience in the face of adversity.

24.6 The Broader Societal Impact of Impulse Control Education

Beyond individual development, the integration of impulse control education into broader societal frameworks contributes to the cultivation of responsible and thoughtful communities. A population equipped with strong impulse control skills is more likely to make collective decisions that prioritize long-term well-being, ethical considerations, and sustainable practices.

24.7 Navigating Challenges and Seeking Support

Despite the emphasis on education, it's essential to acknowledge that impulse control is a skill that individuals may find challenging to master. In such cases, seeking support from educators, counselors, or mental health professionals becomes crucial. Educational institutions and workplaces can play a pivotal role in creating supportive environments that foster the development of impulse control skills.

24.8 Closing Reflections

Education emerges as a transformative force in the journey toward mastering impulse control as a life skill. By integrating cognitive awareness, emotional regulation, critical thinking, and goal-oriented approaches into educational frameworks, individuals are equipped with the tools to navigate the complexities of decision-making. As education continues to evolve, the emphasis on impulse control contributes not only to individual success but also to the creation of resilient, responsible, and forward-thinking societies.

CHAPTER 25

THE FUTURE OF IMPULSE PURCHASING

Predicting Trends and Adapting Strategies

As we stand at the crossroads of technological innovation, evolving consumer behaviors, and societal shifts, the future of impulse purchasing is a dynamic landscape that requires foresight and adaptability. This chapter explores emerging trends, potential trajectories, and strategic considerations for businesses and consumers alike as they navigate the evolving realm of impulse purchasing.

25.1 Technological Advancements Shaping Impulse Purchasing

25.1.1 Artificial Intelligence (AI) and Personalization: The integration of AI into consumer experiences is set to revolutionize impulse purchasing. Advanced algorithms will enable personalized recommendations, leveraging vast datasets to anticipate individual preferences and tailor suggestions in real-time.

25.1.2 Augmented and Virtual Reality Integration: The immersive experiences offered by augmented and virtual reality will likely become integral to impulse purchasing. Consumers may engage with products virtually, fostering a heightened sense of connection and immediacy that transcends traditional online shopping.

25.1.3 Enhanced Data Analytics for Behavioral Insights: Continued advancements in data analytics will provide businesses with deeper insights into consumer behavior. Understanding the intricacies of how individuals make impulsive decisions will enable more targeted and effective marketing strategies.

25.2 Evolving Consumer Values and Preferences

25.2.1 Sustainable and Ethical Impulse Purchasing: The conscientious consumer, driven by environmental and ethical considerations, will shape the future of impulse purchasing. Businesses that align with sustainable practices, transparent sourcing, and ethical values are likely to capture the loyalty of this evolving demographic.

25.2.2 Mindful Consumption Habits: The trend towards mindful consumption will influence impulse purchasing, with consumers prioritizing quality over quantity, seeking products with enduring value, and making intentional choices that align with their values and long-term goals.

25.3 Strategies for Businesses in the Future Landscape

25.3.1 Purpose-Driven Marketing: Businesses that embrace purpose-driven marketing, aligning with social and environmental causes, will resonate with the values of the future consumer. Connecting products to meaningful narratives enhances the appeal of impulsive purchases.

25.3.2 Digital Integration and Seamless Experiences: The convergence of online and offline shopping experiences will continue to define the future of impulse purchasing. Businesses that seamlessly integrate digital and physical platforms, providing a consistent and frictionless journey, will excel in capturing impulsive buying opportunities.

25.3.3 Transparency and Authenticity: Transparent business practices and authentic communication will be paramount. Consumers of the future will demand openness about product origins, manufacturing processes, and the overall impact of their purchases.

25.3.4 Agility and Adaptability: The ability to adapt quickly to changing consumer trends will be a key differentiator. Businesses that demonstrate agility, embrace innovation, and proactively respond to evolving consumer preferences will thrive in the future landscape of impulse purchasing.

25.4 Empowering Consumers in the Decision-Making Process

25.4.1 Education on Mindful Consumption: As consumers become more discerning, education on mindful consumption will play a crucial role. Businesses can contribute by providing resources that empower consumers to make informed, intentional, and responsible impulsive decisions.

25.4.2 Digital Literacy and Awareness: Educating consumers about the digital landscape and the potential influence of algorithms on their choices will enhance digital literacy. Informed consumers are better equipped to navigate online platforms and resist manipulative marketing tactics.

25.5 Ethical Considerations and Responsible Practices

25.5.1 Ethical Marketing Standards: The future demands heightened ethical standards in marketing. Governments, industry associations, and businesses themselves will need to collaborate to establish and enforce ethical guidelines that protect consumers from deceptive practices.

25.5.2 Data Privacy and Security: The responsible handling of consumer data will be non-negotiable. Businesses must prioritize data privacy and security to build and maintain trust with consumers who are increasingly concerned about how their information is used.

25.6 Balancing Innovation with Well-Being

25.6.1 Designing for Well-Being: The future of impulse purchasing requires a delicate balance between innovation and well-being. Businesses should design experiences that enhance consumer well-being, promoting positive and mindful interactions with products and services.

25.6.2 Digital Detox Initiatives: Recognizing the potential negative impact of constant connectivity, businesses may introduce initiatives that encourage digital detox and mindful breaks, fostering a healthier relationship between consumers and technology.

25.7 Collaborative Approaches to Shaping the Future

25.7.1 Industry Collaboration: Businesses, industry associations, and regulatory bodies can collaborate to establish industry-wide standards for responsible impulse marketing. Shared best practices and guidelines can create a more transparent and consumer-friendly landscape.

25.7.2 Consumer-Brand Partnerships: Future consumer-brand relationships may evolve into partnerships where consumers actively engage in the decision-making process. Brands that invite consumer input, co-creation, and feedback will build stronger connections and brand loyalty.

25.8 Closing Thoughts

The future of impulse purchasing is a tapestry woven with technological threads, shifting consumer values, and evolving business strategies. As we navigate this dynamic landscape, businesses and consumers alike have the opportunity to shape a future where impulse purchases are not just moments of spontaneity but intentional, meaningful choices that align with personal values and contribute to a more conscious and sustainable world.

www.ingramcontent.com/pod-product-compliance
Lightning Source LLC
Chambersburg PA
CBHW071208290526
45796CB00008B/187